GREAT ONE-LINERS

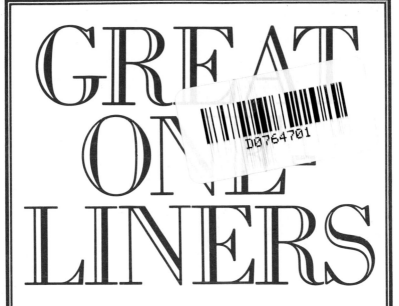

by GENE PERRET,
Bob Hope's Head Comedy Writer,
with Terry Perret Martin

★ ★ ★ ★ ★

Illustrated by Myron Miller

To Bob
Have some
Coughs
Best Wishes
Gene Perret

Sterling Publishing Co., Inc. \ New York

Library of Congress Cataloging-in-Publication Data

Perret, Gene.
    Great one-liners / by Gene Perret with Terry Perret Martin ;
illustrated by Myron Miller.
        p.   cm.
    Includes index.
    Summary: Includes over 1,000 one-line gags from the author and
other personalities, including George Burns, W.C. Fields, Mark Twain,
and Robert Benchley.
    ISBN 0-8069-8514-3
    1. Wit and humor, Juvenile. [1. Wit and humor. 2. Jokes.]
I. Martin, Terry Perret. II. Miller, Myron, 1948–   ill. III. Title.
PN6163.P458   1992
818′.5402—dc20   92-26651
                                              CIP
                                              AC

10 9 8 7 6 5 4 3 2

Published in 1992 by Sterling Publishing Company, Inc.
387 Park Avenue South, New York, N.Y. 10016
© 1992 by Gene Perret
Distributed in Canada by Sterling Publishing
% Canadian Manda Group, P.O. Box 920, Station U
Toronto, Ontario, Canada M8Z 5P9
Distributed in Great Britain and Europe by Cassell PLC
Villiers House, 41/47 Strand, London WC2N 5JE, England
Distributed in Australia by Capricorn Link Ltd.
P.O. Box 665, Lane Cove, NSW 2066
Manufactured in the United States of America
All rights reserved

Sterling ISBN 0-8069-8514-3

to
Kathy,
Bob,
Sue,
and Mike
—*Gene*

★ ★ ★ ★ ★

to
my dear husband, Jack,
who through better or worse,
richer or poorer,
sickness or health . . .
can always make me laugh
—*Terry*

CONTENTS

About One-Liners   7

1. Luck & Laughter   9
Luck • Laughter

2. Family Ties   13
Childhood • Children • Relatives • Pets

3. School Chums & Chumps   21
Education • Dummies • Brains

4. The Sporting Life   27
Football • Baseball • Hockey • Golf • Boxing

5. People We Know & Love—or Don't   37
*Egomaniacs • Bores • Latecomers • Couch
Potatoes • Grouches • Cheapskates • Crazies*

6. Looks *Are* Everything   49
*Fashion • The Worst Dressed • Appearance •
Beauty • Big Eaters • Skinnies • Bodybuilders
• Baldies • Barbers • Hair*

7. Boy Meets Girl, and So On . . .   65
Bachelors • Dating • Marriage

8. Bless Our Happy Home   71
*Money Troubles • Housework • Man Around the
House • Neat Neighbors • Cooking • Kitchen
• Call the Handyman*

9. King of the Road   85
Automobiles • Driving • Traffic

10. I Wonder Where My Luggage Went   93
Travel • Airlines • Hotels

11. I'm in Pretty Good Shape for the Shape I'm In   99
*Health • Hospitals • Doctors, Dentists & Shrinks
• Diets • Exercise*

12. Our World & Welcome to It   109
*Weather • Drought • Earthquakes • Water
Pollution • Air Pollution*

13. Life & Its Aftereffects   119
Birth • Old Age • Death • Spiritual Matters

Index   127

ABOUT ONE-LINERS

Most of us are familiar with the phrase "Good answer." We've heard it shouted by enthusiastic teammates on the television game show "Family Feud." But what is a "good answer?" "Bolivia" might be a good answer, but not in response to the question: Can you name a former President of the United States who did not attend college?

A good answer has to be an appropriate response to a question. An answer can't exist alone. It must be in tandem with a query.

This book is called *Great One-Liners*. A one-liner is a funny, creative, clever response to a situation. Just as an answer can't exist without a corresponding question, so a one-liner can't exist without a set-up.

The set-up can be another sentence, as in Rodney Dangerfield's line:

> My father gave me a bat for Christmas. The first time I tried to play with it, it flew away.

Sometimes, the set-up can be a question, such as:

> QUESTION: What do they call someone who had the stew in the cafeteria today?
>
> ANSWER: An ambulance.

The setup can be a situation. For example, I attended a baseball game with my nephew. One of the home-team players was hit by a pitch on the top of the head. He wasn't seriously injured. As he trotted to first base, my nephew said:

> That's the most wood he's gotten on the ball
> all season.

The set-up can even be self-contained or implied. For example, this line:

> When Noah built the ark, why didn't he
> swat the two flies while he had the chance?

The one-liner, which is a traditional show business joke form, doesn't necessarily mean a one sentence gag. Then why call it a one-liner? Because one of the lines is essential. One of the lines is the funny one. One of the lines is the *punchline*. That's the one line that makes it a joke. That's the line that gives it the name "one-liner."

If that one line is sharp, incisive, creative, clever, funny— then you have a *great* one-liner. I hope that's what you'll enjoy throughout this book.

LUCK & LAUGHTER

ACT 1

*"If you can't make it better,
you can laugh at it."*
—**Erma Bombeck**

LUCK

My luck—I was waiting at the airport when my ship came in. —Henny Youngman

My luck is getting worse and worse. The other night, for instance, I was mugged by a Quaker. —Woody Allen

I don't have any luck. The other day I called Dial-A-Prayer and got a busy signal. —Bob Hope

★ ★ ★ ★ ★

I'm the unluckiest person in the world. As a child, I was allergic to diaper rash.

I'm so unlucky, when I was a kid I had a hobby horse who got hoof-and-mouth disease.

Talk about bad luck. I once drew four aces in a poker game and won $12,000 worth of counterfeit money.

I have terrible luck trying to get a good seat on an airplane. I get sick when I ride forward.

I even have bad luck with things I buy. I bought a very expensive tape recorder. Every time I speak into it, it corrects me.

— ★ —

I bought a very expensive stereo. When I put on my favorite records, it spits them out.

— ★ —

I have bad luck with doctors. The last one I went to wrote out a prescription for me. It was for cigarettes.

— ★ —

Talk about bad luck. I once bought a suit with two pairs of pants and burned a hole in the jacket.

— ★ —

It's bad to suppress laughter: It goes back down and spreads your hips. —Fred Allen

An onion can make people cry—but there has never been a vegetable invented to make them laugh. —Will Rogers

If I get big laughs, I'm a comedian. If I get small laughs, I'm a humorist. If I get no laughs, I'm a singer. —George Burns

Laughter is the sensation of feeling good all over, and showing it principally in one spot. —Josh Billings

Start every day with a smile and get it over with. —W. C. Fields

When my Uncle Willie laughed, his belly shook like Jell-O. Come to think of it, even when Uncle Willie sat still, his belly shook like Jell-O.

As one comedian said, "If my jokes can make just one person laugh this evening, I'll probably be fired before tomorrow evening."

My Aunt Hattie had a loud, raucous laugh that she enjoyed for 57 years, until a family of hyenas sued her for copyright infringement.

Laughter is good for your body, soul, and spirit. It also makes the comedian feel a little better about himself, too.

Laugh and the world laughs with you. Stub your toe and the world laughs whether you do or not.

Aunt Louisa used to laugh like a cackling hen. Uncle Bert would have gotten rid of her except that he needed the eggs.

Love makes the world go 'round, but laughter keeps us all from jumping off.

— ★ —

FAMILY
TIES

ACT
2

*"They call it a family tree
because if you look hard enough,
you'll always find some
sap in it."*

CHILDHOOD

I had a very funny childhood. My mother used to tell me so much about the birds and the bees that it took me years and years to get interested in girls.

—Jack E. Leonard

Each kid nowadays has his own TV, hi-fi, and air-conditioning. Why, when I was a boy, the only time we had air-conditioning was when my mother blew on the minestrone.

—Danny Thomas

I was so ugly as a kid, we never had a jack-o-lantern. They just stuck me in the window. —Rodney Dangerfield

It is good to obey the rules when you're young, so you'll have the strength to break them when you're old.

—Mark Twain

Childhood is a time of rapid changes. Between the ages of twelve and seventeen, a parent can age thirty years.

—Sam Levenson

One day my father took me aside and left me there.

—Jackie Vernon

★ ★ ★ ★ ★

Childhood is a time of life when you have no cares, no worries, no problems, no responsibilities, no money—it sounds a lot like my Uncle Charlie's adulthood.

The first thing that happened in my childhood was the doctor slapped my bottom and made me cry. Then he gave my father the bill and made him cry.

I don't remember if my childhood was happy or not. I was only a kid at the time.

I had a very moving childhood. My parents kept moving without telling me where they were going.

There were always a lot of happy children around our house, which annoyed me. I was an only child.

During my childhood I created imaginary playmates. Then one night they stole all my toys.

This friend of mine had a sheltered childhood. His parents told his teacher, "If he acts up in school, just punish the child next to him."

My mother would try to rock me to sleep as a child, but I kept dodging the rocks.

Some people ask me: "If you had your childhood to live over again, would you do it?" I doubt it—I'm fresh out of diapers.

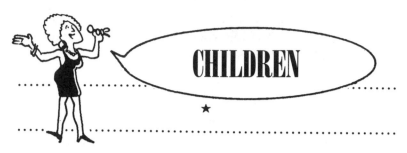

CHILDREN

★

Any mother with half a skull knows that when Daddy's little boy becomes Mommy's little boy, the kid is so wet he's treading water.
—Erma Bombeck

The last thing my kids ever did to earn money was lose their baby teeth.
—Phyllis Diller

My kid said, "Daddy, Mommy said you should take me to the zoo." I said, "If the zoo wants you, let them come and get you."
—Slappy White

Reprimand your child regularly every day. You may not know why, but the kid does.
—Harry Hershfield

Never raise your hand to your children—it leaves your midsection unprotected.
—Fred Allen

How times have changed. Remember 30 years ago when a juvenile delinquent was a kid with an overdue library book?
—Henny Youngman

I had to go to school to see my kid's guidance counselor. They told me my kid was out; he'd be back in one to three years.

—Rodney Dangerfield

★　★　★　★　★

I won't say our kids are bad, but we had to turn down one baby-sitter because she didn't own a crash helmet.

— ★ —

Some of those video games kids play today are so violent. Little girls don't want dolls now unless they blow up other dolls.

— ★ —

One little girl asked a littler girl how old she was. She said, "I think I'm either four or five." The older girl said, "Do you dream about boys?" The little girl said, "No." The older girl said, "You're four."

— ★ —

RELATIVES

★

I slept in the same bed with six brothers. We had a bed wetter. It took us three years to find out who it was.
—Bob Hope

My sister just had a baby. I can't wait to find out if I'm an aunt or an uncle. —Gracie Allen

I grew up with six brothers. That's how I learned to dance—waiting to get into the bathroom. —Bob Hope

My brother is very superstitious—he won't work any week that has a Friday in it. —Milton Berle

My crazy brother-in-law, I wish he would learn a trade, that way we'd know what kind of work he's out of.
—Henny Youngman

GEORGE: *This family of yours—they all lived together?*
GRACIE: *Yes, my father, my uncle, my cousin, my brother, and my nephew used to sleep in one bed, and my—*
GEORGE: *I'm surprised your grandfather didn't sleep with them.*
GRACIE: *Oh, he did, but he died and they made him get up.* —Burns and Allen

★   ★   ★   ★   ★

My parents had a large family. The only way they could afford to feed us all was to start a game of hide-and-seek right before dinner.

— ★ —

There were so many kids in diapers in our family, our house was the only one on the block with a rainbow over it.

— ★ —

My mother always told me that lima beans would put hair on my chest. I don't know how she got my sister to eat them.

— ★ —

My little brother was a mean, vicious child. He would always hit me back.

— ★ —

He has to talk constantly. Once he had laryngitis—he just moved his lips and hired a ventriloquist to travel around with him.

— ★ —

My little brother used to break all my toys, lose parts of all my games, and louse up all my coloring books. I could never catch him at it because I was in my college classes all day.

— ★ —

My brother won't eat any seafood at all. If he comes back in the next life as a pelican, the only time he'll eat is if a cow drowns.

— ★ —

My brother likes all his meat to be cooked extra well done. He doesn't like it to come with a baked potato; he likes it to come with an arson inspector.

— ★ —

My Uncle Newt is as strong as a horse—we just wish he had the I.Q. of one.

— ★ —

I feel sorry for my poor goofy uncle. We can't let him have anything sharp—like a mind.

— ★ —

He's very goofy. When the cuckoo bird comes out of the clock every hour, he tries to pull my uncle back in with him.

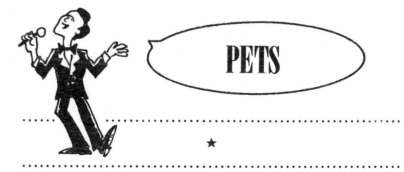

PETS

★

I love a dog. He does nothing for political reasons.
                                            —Will Rogers

If you pick up a starving dog and make him prosperous, he will not bite you. This is the principal difference between a man and a dog.   **—Mark Twain**

I have nothing against dogs. I just hate rugs that go squish-squish.　　　　　　　　　　**—Phyllis Diller**

A boy can learn a lot from a dog: obedience, loyalty and the importance of turning around three times before lying down.　　　　　　　　　　**—Robert Benchley**

I have bad luck with pets. I had a wooden hobby horse when I was a kid. It kicked me in the head.

I once had a dog who was so smart, when we went to obedience school, I was the one on the leash.

I once had a dog who really believed he was man's best friend. He kept borrowing money from me.

I just taught my cocker spaniel how to beg. The other day he came home with $4.37.

The worst thing I ever did was teach my poodle how to beg. Once he learned, he joined the Hari Khrishnas and now he spends all his time at the airport.

We have a very large family dog. He doesn't permit us to sit on the sofa.

— ★ —

This guy said, "Don't worry about the dog. His bark is worse than his bite." I hope he never barks at me because his bite required 14 stitches.

— ★ —

SCHOOL CHUMS & CHUMPS

ACT 3

"*Everybody is ignorant,
only on different subjects.*"
—**Will Rogers**

EDUCATION

★

Training is everything. The peach was once a bitter almond; cauliflower is nothing but cabbage with a college education.
—Mark Twain

I never let my schooling interfere with my education.
—Mark Twain

The teacher told my kid, "An apple a day keeps the doctor away." He said, "What do you got for cops?"
—Rodney Dangerfield

My education was dismal. I went to a series of schools for mentally disabled teachers.
—Woody Allen

When I came home and showed my mother my report card with a mark of 98 in arithmetic, she wanted to know who had gotten the other two points.
—Sam Levenson

CHARLIE MCCARTHY: *I can't take this schoolwork anymore—it's driving me nuts.*

EDGAR BERGEN: *Well, Charlie, I'm sorry, but hard work never killed anyone.*

CHARLIE MCCARTHY: *Still, there's no use in taking chances.*

She doesn't understand the concept of Roman numerals.
She thought we just fought World War Eleven.

—Joan Rivers

I think football games are an important part of college life. Some places it's the only chance the team gets to see the campus.

College football is a money sport. They wanted one kid to drop out of school and sign with the pros, but he couldn't afford the cut in pay.

Spring Break from college—that's a riot with school colors.

Of course, you can't blame them. They study hard. After a tough mid-term exam, it's relaxing to turn over a car.

Students love Parents' Day. It's a chance to get their money without wasting a stamp.

Parents' Day begins with a scavenger hunt. The parents go to their kid's room, move all the junk around, and see who can be the first one to find their kid.

Education can get you the only thing that really matters in today's world—an assigned parking space.

DUMMIES

One dumb guy was elected dog-catcher. He knew he was supposed to catch dogs—but at what? —Milton Berle

My husband, Fang, is so dumb. I once said, "There's a dead bird," and he looked up. —Phyllis Diller

They taught this dumb guy how to run a helicopter. It's up 800 feet. All of a sudden it falls to the ground. I said to him, "What happened?" He says, "It got chilly up there so I turned off the fan." —Henny Youngman

In San Francisco they have a new dumb mime group. They talk! —Henny Youngman

What's on your mind, if you will allow the over-statement? —Fred Allen

★　★　★　★　★

I know a guy who is so dumb he reads mystery novels backwards. He knows who did it, but he doesn't know what they did.

— ★ —

This guy is so dumb he took his dog to obedience school. The dog passed, he flunked.

— ★ —

I have a friend who is so dumb, when he gets amnesia he actually gets smarter.

I knew one guy who was so dumb he had his address tattooed to his forehead. That way if he got lost, he could mail himself home.

This guy is so lame-brained, he parts his hair in the middle so he won't have to remember each morning which side he parts it on.

One guy was so dumb he had to have "left" and "right" tattooed on his toes so he would know which feet his shoes go on. Now, if he could only learn to read.

One guy was so dumb he lost his shoes one day because he put them on the wrong feet. Then he couldn't remember whose feet he put them on.

One friend of mine was so stupid he had to take the I.Q. test twice to get it up to a whole number.

Talk about stupid! Someone gave this guy a pair of cuff links. He didn't have a shirt with french cuffs, so he had his wrists pierced.

This guy is stupid. His hobby used to be catching butterflies, but he got tired digging up worms to use for bait.

I had a friend who was so dumb he mixed baby powder with water and tried to get a little brother.

— ★ —

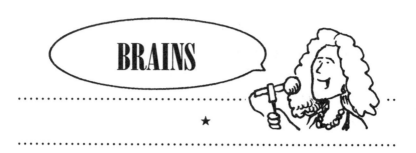

BRANS

I am smart. I know a lot, I just can't think of it.
—Morey Amsterdam

Smartness runs in my family. When I went to school I was so smart my teacher was in my class for five years.
—Gracie Allen

You know horses are smarter than people. You never heard of a horse going broke betting on people.
—Will Rogers

It is so simple to be smart. Just think of something stupid to say, then say the opposite.
—Sam Levenson

I know this guy who's such a brain, if he doesn't know the answer, there isn't one.

I went to school with a kid who was so smart, the only time he got an answer wrong, they had to go back and change the question.

— ★ —

We had a kid in our class that we used to call "The Brain." Not because he was smart, but because he was grey and lumpy and shaped like a big cauliflower.

— ★ —

THE SPORTING LIFE

ACT 4

"Sports is the only entertainment where,
no matter how many times you go back,
you'll never know the ending."

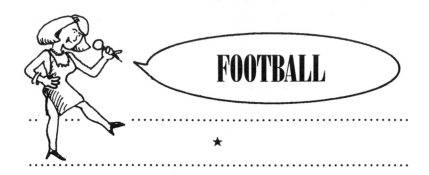

FOOTBALL

The Rose Bowl is the only bowl I've seen that I didn't have to clean.　　　　　　　　　**—Erma Bombeck**

I'm a football fan, but I think there are too many games on over the holidays. At our Thanksgiving dinner, Dolores passed me the turkey and I spiked it.
　　　　　　　　　　　　　　　　　　—Bob Hope

Football is quite a sport. Every weekend they have to get up early, get hyped up for the game, get their uniforms on—and that's only the fans.

Everybody gets dressed in crazy costumes to go to football games nowadays. I've been to games where the only two creatures in the entire stadium who looked normal were the team mascots.

The fans have a good time. I get the feeling that if football were banned, the fans would still show up every weekend anyway.

Football is getting rough. You have to wear shoulder pads, a face mask, and a helmet—and that's just to sit in the stands.

Football players say the fans are so noisy that they can't even hear themselves think. At most, that would affect maybe one or two players on the team.

They have more fights in the stands each Sunday than Muhammad Ali had in his entire career.

At the Los Angeles Coliseum one Sunday, eight fights broke out in the stands before they realized the Raiders were playing an away game that weekend.

One football fan always buys two seats—one to sit in and one to use as a weapon when the fight breaks out.

Everybody knows how rowdy the fans get. The vendors go up and down the aisles hollering, "Peanuts, popcorn, bandages. . . ."

Football is a violent sport. They do things in this sport that you get penalized for in hockey.

It's getting worse, too. They used to carry the players off the field on a stretcher; now they use a shopping bag.

This one guy was a hard-nosed football player. He was respected, he was feared, he was avoided—and that was in his own huddle.

During his playing days, he would kick, scratch, claw—do anything to gain an advantage. It got so his teammates asked that he eat in another dining room.

— ★ —

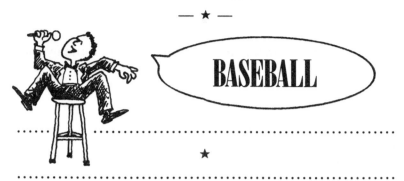

BASEBALL

★

Last Christmas, my father gave me a bat. First time I tried to play with it, it flew away.

—Rodney Dangerfield

A friend gave me seats to the World Series. From where I sat, the game was just a rumor. —Henny Youngman

Some of our hitters are so bad they can strike out on two pitches. —Milton Berle

★ ★ ★ ★ ★

I like baseball as a sport, because in baseball when you hit a ball into the stands you just forget about it. In golf, you have to go looking for it.

— ★ —

Baseball is easier than golf. In baseball, you hit the ball and someone else chases it.

— ★ —

I played on a bad baseball team when I was a kid. The only thing our shortstop caught all year was mononucleosis.

— ★ —

One kid on my team got beaned the other day. The coach said it's the most wood he got on the ball all season.

— ★ —

We got very few hits. If anybody on our team reached first base, he had to stop and ask for directions.

— ★ —

We had such bad hitters. On our team a foul ball was considered a rally.

— ★ —

We were losing one game 126 to 0, but we weren't worried. We hadn't had our turn at bat yet.

— ★ —

We only had one victory all season, and that was when the other team didn't show up.

. . . We won 1 to 0 in the bottom of the 12th.

— ★ —

We had such a bad team that every time we took the field our manager got fined for littering.

— ★ —

Baseball is very special to me because it has changed so little over the years. It's a lot like my bank account.

— ★ —

Baseball players make a lot of money nowadays. Even guys who don't make the team are getting seven figures.

— ★ —

Baseball players are getting too rich. They hit the ball now and have their chauffeurs run to first for them.

— ★ —

The cost of high baseball salaries is being passed on to the fans. You can't buy a hot dog at the ballpark now unless you can find a co-signer.

. . . if you want mustard and relish, you have to mortgage your house.

— ★ —

A player was just signed for over $3 million a season. If I made that much money, I wouldn't steal second. I'd buy it.

— ★ —

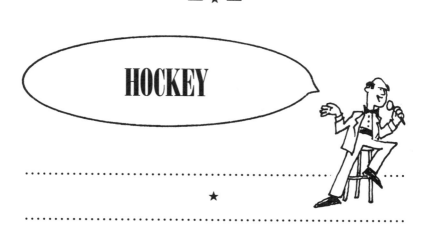

HOCKEY

★

Our team lives hockey, it dreams hockey, it eats hockey. Now if it could only play hockey.   —Milton Berle

★   ★   ★   ★   ★

Hockey is a game where you take a stick and hit either the puck, or anyone who has touched the puck.

— ★ —

Most fans agree that hockey is the fastest game played today. And if any fans don't agree, you hit them across the back of the neck with a hockey stick.

— ★ —

Hockey is a rough and tumble game and tempers do flare occasionally, but wouldn't life be much better today if the world had been designed with a penalty box?

— ★ —

When I was a kid, I thought hockey players who were sent to the penalty box had to sit there until their fathers got home from work.

. . . come to think of it, that's not a bad idea.

— ★ —

There are only three ways to play hockey: rough, rougher, and "I'll help you look for your teeth if you'll help me look for mine."

— ★ —

Most hockey players aren't big, either. Their bodies are just large enough to carry all the black and blue marks they get in a game.

— ★ —

Put it on ice and it's called "hockey." Put it in a department store and it's called the "January White Sale."

— ★ —

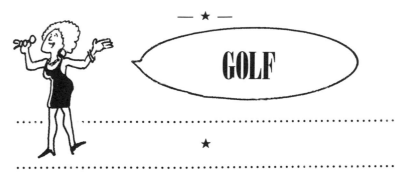

GOLF

★

To me, golf was something you did with your hands while you talked. Unless you smoked—then you never had to leave the clubhouse.
                                              —Erma Bombeck

Income tax has made more liars out of the American people than golf. —Will Rogers

Golf is the only game, outside of solitaire, where you play alone. What you do with your ball hasn't got anything to do with what the other fellow does with his. It's solitaire, only quieter. —Will Rogers

Would you believe there are 3,000 miniature golf courses in the city of Los Angeles. Half of America is bent over. —Will Rogers

Give me my golf clubs, the fresh air and a beautiful woman as a partner—and you can have the golf clubs and the fresh air. —George Burns

You don't have to keep score when you play golf with Jerry Ford. You just look back along the fairway and count the wounded. —Bob Hope

They have some new equipment in golf now that favors seniors. Like that long putter you put right under your chin. You can putt and take a nap at the same time.

— ★ —

My uncle has a different name for golf—connect the sand traps.

. . . He can play five or six rounds of golf without having the ball touch grass once.

— ★ —

Arnold Palmer makes millions of dollars playing golf, and that's not counting all those dimes he's collected picking up other people's ball markers.

— ★ —

Jerry Ford changed the game of golf. When you're in his foursome, you don't think of the bunkers as hazards. They're more like a form of protection.

— ★ —

You know, people don't mind getting hit by Jerry Ford. They're just glad he didn't take up bowling.

— ★ —

I put the "pu" in "pugilism."   —Bob Hope

That fight was so short that when they raised the winner's arm, I thought it was a deodorant commercial.
                                           —Slappy White

I went to the boxing matches the other night, and a hockey game broke out.   —Rodney Dangerfield

★   ★   ★   ★   ★

I was a pretty good fighter once. I used to be able to take a good punch. The only problem was I'd take it 30 or 40 times a round.

— ★ —

I used to run three or four miles right before a fight. But my opponent always caught me and beat me up anyway.

— ★ —

I was noted for my fancy footwork as a boxer. I was disqualified from 12 fights for kicking.

I always had special boxing shorts made when I got into the ring. I needed something to go with the yellow streak down my back.

There was one thing I never got to see in my boxing career—the end of the first round.

I had to give up boxing for financial reasons. I couldn't afford to buy any more smelling salts.

I was a bad boxer. I got knocked out three times when I was shadowboxing.

I couldn't punch my way out of a paper bag, which is what I wore to my fights since I couldn't afford a robe.

It's crazy when you figure boxers get all that money for fighting and hockey players do it every night for free.

I have a problem with boxing. I don't understand any sport where a guy who makes eleven million dollars is called "the Loser."

Boxing is a funny sport. They say, "May the better man win," and then when he does, they attack the referee.

PEOPLE WE
KNOW &
LOVE
—OR DON'T

ACT
5

*"If you can't say something good
about someone, sit right here by me."*
—Alice Roosevelt Longworth

EGOMANIACS

I talk to myself because I like dealing with a better class of people. —Jackie Mason

This guy is such an egotist, the towels in his bathroom are marked "His" and "His." —Milton Berle

He is a very religious man. He worships himself. —Jack E. Leonard

The last time I saw him, he was walking down Lover's Lane holding his own hand. —Fred Allen

★ ★ ★ ★ ★

An egomaniac is a guy who thinks he's always right and he's wrong.

— ★ —

I hate egotists. They all think they're as good as I am.

— ★ —

I dreamed I was the Ruler of the Entire World last night. When my alarm clock went off, I had it beheaded.

— ★ —

I know a guy who thinks he's God's gift to women. And all the women are hoping the gift is returnable.

— ★ —

If this guy's head was any bigger, his hat size would be the same as his zip code.

This guy's head would swell up so often he had to wear an expandable hat.

He once said to me, "I'm the greatest thing on earth." I said, "You've got yourself confused with a circus."

I knew one egomaniac who actually thought he was humble. He used to say: "Some geniuses are conceited, but I'm not."

One friend of mine used to look in the mirror and think he was handsome. He was either an egomaniac or near-sighted.

BORES

Everyone says he has a dull personality. That's not true— he has no personality at all. —Morey Amsterdam

The town was so dull that when the tide went out, it refused to come back. —Fred Allen

★ ★ ★ ★ ★

This guy is so dull, at parties people would mistake him for the cheese dip.

This guy is so boring, the most excitement he's ever had in his life was once when he entered a fingernail-growing contest.

. . . He lost. He said the most he could ever grow was ten.

Talk about dull! This guy has the personality of a soup spoon.

. . . and gets invited to just about as many parties.

This guy is so dull, he once joined a computer dating service and they matched him with lard.

This guy is not exciting. Getting your toe stuck in the bathtub faucet is more fun than being with him.

This guy is so dull, when he goes to a party, the party goes somewhere else.

Anyone who says nothing exists in a vacuum, has never seen this guy's personality.

This guy has all the excitement of a wet wick at a fireworks display.

— ★ —

This man is dull. He was once almost attacked by a shark. The shark circled him three times and lost interest.

— ★ —

LATECOMERS

I have the feeling there's a correlation between getting up in the morning and getting up in the world.

—Milton Berle

I know one guy who arrives late for everything. In fact, the rule of thumb is: if you don't get there before he does, there's no sense going.

— ★ —

This kid I know arrives late for everything. He was three years old at his first birthday party.

— ★ —

This boy has always been late for everything. His twin brother is six months older than he is.

— ★ —

This guy is always late—even for ball games. He thinks the words to the National Anthem are ". . . and the home of the brave play ball."

This guy is always late. He threw a New Year's Eve party for all his friends last March 15th.

This guy arrives at parties so late he has to bring his own cheese dip.

— ★ —

This guy arrives so late at parties that by the time he throws his coat in the bedroom, the host and hostess are generally asleep in it.

— ★ —

All through his education, the only time he wasn't late for school was when he was absent.

. . . and he would've been late for that if he could have been there.

— ★ —

If you want this guy to be someplace on time, it's safer to invite someone else.

— ★ —

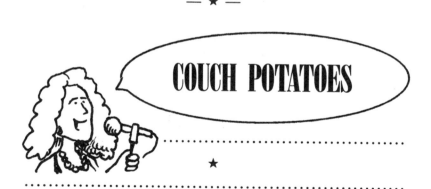

COUCH POTATOES

★

Fang can't stand to see trash and garbage lying around the house. He can't stand the competition.
                                                    —Phyllis Diller

I should have suspected my husband was lazy when his mother told me on our wedding day: "I'm not losing a son; I'm gaining a couch."
                                                    —Phyllis Diller

I can't go to work because I have trouble with my back. I can't get it off the bed. —Jackie Mason

There is no radical cure for laziness, but starvation will come the nearest to it. —Josh Billings

The laziest man I ever met put popcorn in his pancakes so they would turn over by themselves. —W. C. Fields

I do some work around the house once in a while. The last time I worked up a sweat, my wife didn't wash my work shirt, she framed it.

I'm so lazy I never turn the ball game on until the second inning. I'm afraid I might be a little early and have to stand for the National Anthem.

I had to get a new alarm clock. It flashes a light, rings a bell, then gives me mouth-to-mouth resuscitation.

I know a guy who is so lazy he likes to do absolutely nothing at all. He just closes his eyes and pretends he's a politician.

He spends his entire day half asleep. He just leaves word for his family not to move him at all unless he's on fire.

His biggest decision is deciding whether he wants salt or pepper on his eggs in the morning. He's too lazy to shake both.

He's too lazy to even wind a self-winding watch. He slips it on his dog's tail and then makes a fuss over him.

The only way he brushes his teeth is barefoot on the cold marble floor. He figures it's less work if he just holds the brush still and lets his teeth chatter.

He taught his dog to fetch, but he's so lazy he also taught him to throw the stick too.

GROUCHES

Our new neighbor is so grouchy. He moved into the neighborhood the other day and was fired on by the Welcome Wagon. —Milton Berle

★ ★ ★ ★ ★

I'm such a grouch in the morning, not even the milkman will come near the house. He mails us our milk.

I have a neighbor who is a total grouch. We had a block party once—we held it on another street.

This woman is such a grouch, even the paperboy won't go near her. He calls on the phone and reads the paper to her.

— ★ —

I'm very grouchy when I wake up in the morning. The safest way to get me out of bed is to step on my back and pick me up by the claws.

I know a guy who was such a miserable grouch that at his funeral, the only pallbearers they could get were six guys who had never met him.

I knew one kid who was miserable about everything. At his birthday party, he didn't blow out the candles—he chased them home.

I knew one woman who had such a terrible frown on her face all the time that when she put on her make-up, it curdled.

This woman is such a grouch, no one goes near her. The stork left her baby two blocks away, and she had to go pick it up.

— ★ —

CHEAPSKATES

I took my date to dinner last night. She was so excited, she dropped her tray.
—Jack Benny

Fang took the entire family out for coffee and donuts the other night. The kids enjoyed it. It was the first time they'd ever given blood. —Phyllis Diller

This guy is so cheap he won't even eat in the sun for fear his shadow will ask him for a bite. —Jack Benny

Cheap? His hearing aid is on a party line.
—Henny Youngman

★ ★ ★ ★ ★

This friend of mine is the cheapest man I've ever known. He still has the first dollar he ever borrowed.

— ★ —

This guy is so cheap, he not only has the first dollar he ever made, but also the arm of the man who handed it to him.

— ★ —

This guy is so cheap, he always leaves a 20-percent tip—20 percent of what anybody else would leave.

— ★ —

My wife says I'm so cheap I only open my wallet for two reasons—to put money in and to let the guard out on his day off.

— ★ —

It's not that I'm cheap. I just hate to give money away after I've memorized the serial number.

— ★ —

I had a friend who was so cheap, he borrowed a suit to be buried in.

— ★ —

This guy owes so much money to so many people, his answering machine just says, "Hi, your check's in the mail."

He's so cheap he'd like to put a few bucks into the stock market, but all his money is sewn into his mattress.

— ★ —

This guy is so cheap he won't buy deodorant. He buys a soap that odor-proofs the body for 12 hours, and keeps turning the clock back.

— ★ —

I was on an airline that was so cheap, we had to fly at a low altitude. The captain explained if we go any higher, the sun melts the wax wings.

— ★ —

This airline was so cheap, instead of a movie, they put on a high-school play.

— ★ —

I was on an airline that was so cheap, when they rolled those little steps away, the plane fell over on its side.

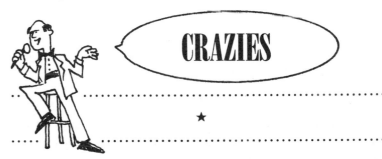

CRAZIES

★

I just read that one out of every four people is mentally unbalanced. Try it—think of three of your best friends. If they seem all right to you—you're the one.
—Slappy White

There is a thin line between genius and insanity. I have erased that line. —Oscar Levant

★　★　★　★　★

They asked my Uncle Wally if anybody in his family suffers from insanity. He said, "No, they all seem to be enjoying it."

People considered my Uncle Mort crazy because he always wore one red sock and one blue one—instead of trousers and a suit coat.

We had one guy in our neighborhood who thought he was a rooster. It was sad. The day after he died, everyone overslept.

I had a friend who was a paranoid-schizophrenic. He always thought he was following himself.

One friend of mine always thought he was too short to amount to anything. I convinced him that was crazy. When he left my house that night, a cat ate him.

I had an aunt who thought she was the Queen of England. I would have told her how insane that was, but I didn't want to blow my chance at Knighthood.

I had one aunt who thought she was the Goodyear blimp. Sure, it sounds crazy to you, but she got to see a lot of football games for free.

ACT
6

LOOKS
ARE
EVERYTHING

*"You look like a million bucks
—all wrinkled and green."*
—Henny Youngman

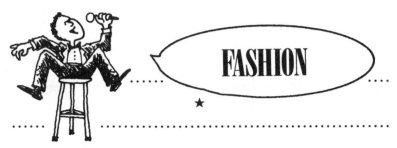

FASHION

Heaven knows, I try to bend the dictates of fashion, but I'm a loser. When I grew my own bustle, they went out of style. —Erma Bombeck

Clothes make the man. Naked people have little or no influence in society. —Mark Twain

It's hard to buy a negligee in my size. I wear a Junior Mister. —Phyllis Diller

I'll never forget my first fur. It was a modest little stole. Modest? People thought I was wearing anchovies. —Phyllis Diller

I base most of my fashion taste on what doesn't itch. —Gilda Radner

★   ★   ★   ★   ★

This girl's dress was tighter than my skin. I can sit down in my skin.

I don't know where the girls get some of those bikinis. No one knows where they buy them; they're not big enough to hold a label.

Dress shoes nowadays are ones that don't have "Reebok" written across them.

There are three categories of clothes to wear to parties now—formal, semi-formal and sweat.

I went to a cocktail party the other night and I felt terribly overdressed. I was the only one wearing a velour warm-up suit.

He always had a sharp crease in his trousers—even when he wasn't wearing any.

He wore a shirt and tie everywhere—even into the shower.

He not only had his shoes shined each morning, but his socks and feet, too.

At his own funeral he made the undertaker feel underdressed.

He wore a shirt, tie, and business suit no matter where he went or what he did. It made swimming laps at the YMCA a little messy.

He was such a meticulous dresser—if you saw a thread hanging from his clothing, chances are it was supposed to be there.

He was always careful about his clothing. As an infant, he used to change his own diapers.

THE WORST DRESSED

Last Saturday my husband wore sneakers, sweat socks, khakis with paint all over them, and a white shirt open at the collar with the undershirt showing—I was too embarrassed to introduce him to the bride.

—Phyllis Diller

Once I opened a closet and a moth had eaten my sports jacket. He was lying on the floor nauseous.

—Woody Allen

I wasn't dressed properly because you don't wear argyles with dark blue. I had on dark blue socks and an argyle suit.

—Woody Allen

★　★　★　★　★

I can be a neat dresser. When we go formal, I insist that the tuxedo trousers just touch the top of my sandals.

I dress so badly, my wife doesn't want people to know I'm her husband. When I open the door for her, she tips me.

One of my friends is even worse. His pants are so baggy in the seat and so droopy in the knees that from the side he looks like the Mark of Zorro.

His sweater has every color in the rainbow and even a few colors rainbows won't wear in public.

— ★ —

He took some of his old sweaters and threw them in the Goodwill bin. The bin threw them back out.

— ★ —

For such a well-to-do man, he dresses terribly. He never lets success go to his clothing.

— ★ —

Nothing he wears ever matches. We think he buys all his clothes at Hart, Schaffner, Barnum and Bailey.

— ★ —

APPEARANCE

★

My nose was so big when I was a kid, I thought it was a third arm.   —David Brenner

"Hey, where are my glasses?"
"On your nose."
"Be more specific."   —Jimmy Durante

You won't believe this—but I was an ugly baby. I was so ugly my mother used to diaper my face. —Jackie Mason

I'm the only woman who can walk Central Park at night and reduce the crime rate.   —Phyllis Diller

When I go to the beach, even the tide won't come in.
                    —Phyllis Diller

She had the biggest overbite in Brooklyn. She used to eat a piece of toast and finish the outer edges first.

—Woody Allen

I knew a girl who was so heavy that when her husband carried her over the threshold, he had to make two trips.

Talk about heavy. She's the only woman I know who looks the same sitting down as she does standing up.

Her husband is as heavy as she is. They had to be married in adjoining churches.

My friend is so heavy, when she visits Rhode Island, parts of her hang over into Connecticut.

This woman is very popular at Church picnics. She can provide the entire congregation with shade.

This woman was so heavy, last month she lost four girdles— while she was wearing them.

This woman was so overweight, when she took her girdle off her feet disappeared.

He was big even as a child. It took them until he was six years old to figure out he wasn't twins.

He's so big he has to have all his clothes custom-made. Not by a tailor—by a contractor.

— ★ —

His nose doesn't look like a nose. It looks like something you'd carry spare parts in.

— ★ —

I look so awful in the morning, I had the mirror put on the inside of the medicine chest.

— ★ —

★

My wife went to the beauty parlor and got a mud pack. For two days she looked nice. Then the mud fell off.
—Henny Youngman

I remember how excited I got one day when I discovered a cosmetic stick that would erase away wrinkles—I erased my entire face. —Erma Bombeck

I spent seven hours in a beauty shop—and that was for the estimate. —Phyllis Diller

Most people get an appointment at a beauty parlor—I was committed. —Phyllis Diller

★   ★   ★   ★   ★

Beauty is only skin deep, which is all right—that's as far as most of us can see anyway.

— ★ —

Some say that beauty is only skin deep, but ugly goes all the way to the bone.

— ★ —

True beauty can be a curse. Unfortunately, I'm only a mild invective.

— ★ —

I knew a girl who went to beauty college and flunked "cosmetics." They let her take a "make-up" exam.

— ★ —

Some women take over an hour to put on their natural beauty.

— ★ —

Men are going to beauty parlors now too. It's the macho thing to do. All over the country I can just hear guys saying, "I'm gonna run down to the corner and get a couple of beers and a body wax."

— ★ —

BIG EATERS

★

Fang says he eats a lot to settle his nerves. I said, "Have you seen where they're settling?" —**Phyllis Diller**

My favorite meal is breakfast, lunch, dinner, and in-between. —Totie Fields

My wife is so fat that every time she gets into a cab, the driver rushes her to the hospital. —Dave Barry

I won't tell you how much I weigh, but don't get in an elevator with me—unless you're going down. —Jack E. Leonard

She's so fat, she's got more chins than the Chinese telephone directory. —Joan Rivers

This guy eats all the time. He had two teeth pulled last week. They weren't decayed, just exhausted.

This guy has such an appetite, he can eat an entire cake by himself—while it's baking.

They say this guy eats like a bird. That means when he gets hungry enough, he'll swoop down and scoop up an entire baby goat.

This guy reminds you of a chipmunk—except instead of storing food up for the winter, he stores food up for lunch.

— ★ —

This guy has the appetite of a shark who is going on Weight Watchers tomorrow.

— ★ —

What an appetite! This guy will eat anything that's standing still. He'll eat anything that's moving, too, only it takes him longer.

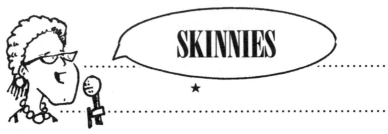

SKINNIES

★

If it weren't for my Adam's apple, I'd have no shape at all.
—Phyllis Diller

There was a time when I had a 23" waist. I was 10 years old—my measurements were 23-23-23.
—Erma Bombeck

I ate more than you for breakfast. —Jackie Gleason

This man was so skinny, he was a waste of skin.
—Fred Allen

This girl was so skinny, she once got a tattoo and it had to be continued on a friend.

My wife is so skinny, when she wears a fur coat she looks like a pipe cleaner.

I'll give you an idea how skinny this girl is: she can put her slacks on over her head.

My girl is so skinny, when she wears a ring, it can easily slip off her finger—in either direction.

This girl is so thin, she wore a strapless gown once and I don't know what held it up—or why!

This girl is so skinny, she's the only one in her family with a fur coat. She made it herself—skinned a caterpillar.

This girl is so skinny, she once wore a green dress and everyone wanted to know if she was poisonous.

— ★ —

My girl is so skinny, for a masquerade party she put on a fur hat and fuzzy slippers and went as a Q-tip.

— ★ —

★

This kid has muscles everywhere. He can bench-press 250 pounds—with his eyebrows. —Bob Hope

This guy has muscles in places where I don't even have places. —Bob Hope

★ ★ ★ ★ ★

This is one big guy. He has a ship tattooed on his chest—actual size.

— ★ —

School kids nowadays are taking steroids to grow muscles. They enter their freshman year as a nerd and graduate as a Neanderthal.

Is that guy big and strong or what? I've seen John Deere tractors that weren't built that well.

— ★ —

Look at the size of this guy. I've heard a lot of sonic booms. This is the first time I've ever met one.

— ★ —

Look at the size of this boy and this is just the basic model. All of his real muscles he left packed in his gym bag.

— ★ —

My gym teacher said I could be a real muscleman if I wanted to be. He says I have the head for it.

— ★ —

I tried to go to a gym to build up my physique, but it was too much work. So I just gave my instructor the money and asked him to walk me home at night.

— ★ —

Barbers don't charge him for cutting his hair. They charge him for searching for it. —Henny Youngman

There's one good thing about being bald. It's neat.
—Milton Berle

I'm not exactly bald—I simply have an exceptionally large part. —Jack E. Leonard

Because of my father, I'm going bald. When I was a kid, my father got mad and he used to hit me in the head and he loosened my hair. Now, it's falling out. —Sid Caesar

His hair is getting thinner—but who wants fat hair.
—Milton Berle

★　★　★　★　★

There's only one real cure for baldness—hair.

— ★ —

There's a good reason why bald people don't get dandruff—they have no place to keep it.

— ★ —

My uncle bought a cheap toupee made out of dog hair, but every time he passes a fire hydrant, one end of it lifts up.

— ★ —

My Uncle Wally said he never saw a bald dog, so he injected himself with Cocker Spaniel hormones. Now he's got a nice head of wavy hair, but his ears keep flopping in his food.

. . . he's also got fleas.

. . . and Aunt Mabel won't let him up on the couch.

— ★ —

Some people don't mind being bald and others do. Men generally handle it better than women.

— ★ —

My Uncle Wally tried to invent a potion that would grow hair on a billiard ball, but he made a mistake. Now his head is covered with green felt.

. . . and instead of dandruff, he has chalk dust.

— ★ —

My Uncle Wally is so bald he has to buy hats with non-skid sweatbands.

— ★ —

BARBERS

★

The barber held up a mirror to see if I liked my new haircut. I said, "Make it a little longer." —Jackie Kahane

That's a great barber shop. I used to go there for a shave and an overcoat. —Milton Berle

When one barber shaves another, who does the talking? —Milton Berle

★   ★   ★   ★   ★

My buddy puts so much grease in his hair, when he sits in the chair the barber says, "Do you want a haircut or an oil change?"

— ★ —

My barber said, "Why don't you try something different for a change?" I said, "Okay, this time give me a *good* haircut."

— ★ —

I always laugh at my barber's jokes. After all, he does have a razor in his hand.

— ★ —

My barber has a very sharp wit. I just wish he had scissors to match.

— ★ —

I asked my barber why he ties that cloth around my neck so tight. He said, "In case I cut you, it doubles as a tourniquet."

— ★ —

My barber said he hates the sight of blood, so he puts a blindfold on when he shaves me.

— ★ —

I told my barber to be careful while he was working on me; I didn't want him to cut my ear off. He said, "Don't worry. I have a drawer full of spares."

— ★ —

My barber said, "I've been in business 35 years and have never lost an ear." I said, "That's nice, but how about your customers?"

— ★ —

I sat down in my barber's chair and said, "Make me look handsome." He said, "I'm a barber, not a faith healer."

— ★ —

★

I comb my hair with an electric toothbrush.
—Phyllis Diller

I said to my hairdresser, "What would look good on me?"
He said, "A Los Angeles Rams football helmet."

—Phyllis Diller

I always wanted to turn to my hairdresser and say, "If I
wanted hair the consistency and style of a steel helmet, I
would have been a Viking." —Erma Bombeck

He wore his hair in a ponytail, which somehow seemed to go
with the rest of his personality.

Her ponytail was too tight. Every time she blinked her
mouth popped open.

Everyone told her her ponytail was too tight. One's ears
should not touch in the back of one's head.

She wore so much hair spray that when you ran your fingers
through her hair, you had to count them afterwards.

She wore so much hair spray that once she bumped her head
and fractured three curls.

BOY MEETS GIRL & SO ON . . .

ACT 7

"*Will Rogers said he never met a man he didn't like. But then, Will Rogers never had to date one.*"
—Linda Perret

BACHELORS

★

A bachelor believes that one can live as cheaply as two.
—Milton Berle

A bachelor is a guy who hasn't let a woman pin anything on him since he wore diapers.
—Milton Berle

I belong to Bridegrooms Anonymous. Whenever I feel like getting married, they send over a lady in a housecoat and hair curlers to burn my toast for me.
—Dick Martin

★ ★ ★ ★ ★

Some say a bachelor is a man who has never made the same mistake once.

— ★ —

Men are bachelors by choice. Sometimes it's their choice; sometimes the choice of the women they meet.

— ★ —

Bachelorhood is tough. You have to hog your own covers.

— ★ —

Bachelorhood is one way of keeping all that alimony money for yourself.

— ★ —

When it comes to marriage, a bachelor is a man who gets cold feet and no one to keep them warm in bed.

— ★ —

A bachelor never knows the joy of wedded bliss; never knows the joy of having children; never knows the joy of raising a family. But he does know the joy of never knowing those other joys.

— ★ —

Bachelorhood means you can mow the lawn when *you* want to.

— ★ —

A married man is the head of his household, but a bachelor has total control of his own television remote control device.

— ★ —

I have no self-confidence. When girls tell me yes, I tell them to think it over.   —Rodney Dangerfield

One woman I was dating said, "Come on over, there's nobody home." I went over—nobody was home.
                    —Rodney Dangerfield

I don't date women my own age—there are no women my own age.   —George Burns

I asked my date what she wanted to drink. She said, "Oh, I guess I'll have champagne." I said, "Guess again."
                    —Slappy White

I went on a first date with one girl. She ran into a guy she used to know. She introduced me to him. She said, "Steve, this is Rodney. Rodney, this is good-bye."

—Rodney Dangerfield

My daughter brought home a date who was so ugly, I said, "You can marry him if you want, but I'm not going to the wedding unless he agrees to wear a veil, too."

— ★ —

Falling in love is like buying a new car—and marriage is the first scratch.

— ★ —

HER FATHER: Have my daughter home by midnight.
HER DATE: Why? Does she turn into a pumpkin?

— ★ —

I used to date our town librarian. I asked her to marry me once and she said, "Sssshhhh."

— ★ —

I took the daughter of the school librarian to the Junior Prom. If I didn't have her back by midnight, I got fined a nickel a minute.

. . . I not only had to get her home on time, but return her to the same shelf from which I picked her up.

— ★ —

I've got a friend who'll chase anything in a skirt, which is why our school band got rid of their bagpipe uniforms.

— ★ —

MARRIAGE

★

My husband has always felt that marriage and a career don't mix—that is why he's never worked.
—Phyllis Diller

I should have known something was wrong with my first wife when I brought her home to meet my parents and they approved. —Woody Allen

My wife is an immature woman. I would be home in the bathroom taking a bath, and my wife would walk in whenever she felt like it and sink my boats.
—Woody Allen

Did you ever notice when a guy opens a car door for his wife, either the car is new or the wife is.
—Woody Woodbury

I haven't spoken to my wife in weeks—I didn't want to interrupt her. —Henny Youngman

My wife has a slight impediment in her speech—every once in a while she stops to breathe.
—Henny Youngman

Fang and I are always fighting. When we get up in the morning, we don't kiss; we touch gloves. —Phyllis Diller

★ ★ ★ ★ ★

My wife loves to argue. When I said "I do," she said, "Oh no you don't."

A good marriage lasts forever and a bad one seems to.

— ★ —

Most people get married because they're hopelessly in love. Then it's a toss-up which lasts longer—the love or the hopelessness.

— ★ —

When we celebrated our 50th wedding anniversary, I said, "Honey, it just doesn't seem like 50 years." She said, "Speak for yourself."

— ★ —

Some people say they don't believe in marriage because it's only a piece of paper. So is money, but we all believe in that.

— ★ —

EVE: Adam, are you seeing another woman?
ADAM: What do you think—I'm made of ribs?

— ★ —

My wife and I have an agreement where we never go to sleep at night angry at each other. We've been awake now for seven months.

— ★ —

BLESS OUR HAPPY HOME

ACT
8

"*Home, nowadays, is a place where
part of the family waits till
the rest of the family brings the car back.*"
—**Earl Wilson**

MONEY TROUBLE

★

GEORGE: *Rich, me? No, I'm a pauper.*
GRACIE: *Congratulations. Boy or girl?*
—Burns and Allen

We had so little to eat one year, I forgot how to swallow.
—Joey Bishop

My landlord said, "I'm going to have to raise your rent." I said, "I wish you would because I sure can't raise it."
—Slappy White

The neighborhood where I grew up was so poor, they tore it down and put up a slum. —Danny Thomas

★ ★ ★ ★ ★

The neighborhood I lived in was so poor, we couldn't even afford neighbors.

— ★ —

We lived in an apartment house where the walls were so thin, you knew everything the neighbors were saying—by reading their lips.

— ★ —

We had a fire in our bathroom one night. Fortunately, it didn't spread to the house.

— ★ —

We were so poor, when the wolf came to our door, he had to bring his own lunch.

Whoever said "Whatever goes up must come down" has not bothered to check the price of houses lately.

At one time you had to be smart to come in out of the rain. Nowadays you have to be rich.

Everyone should be able to have roof over their head. If you also want walls and a floor you may be getting out of your price range.

Women are worried about who's going to care for their kids while they work. That shouldn't be a problem much longer. With today's housing costs even the kids will have to find jobs.

Every young family needs two incomes now. One for food and one for shelter. Clothing you get from your older brothers and sisters.

Sporting events are getting expensive. Soon the fans will have to decide whether to go to the game or send their kids to college.

When I first heard how badly the stock market was doing, I tried to call my broker, but his ledge was busy.

The stock market went down fast and a lot of people in Beverly Hills lost quite a bit of money. People there now have their chauffeurs drop them off at a soup kitchen.

HOUSEWORK

★

I said to my wife, "Where do you want to go for our anniversary?" She said, "I want to go somewhere I've never been before." I said, "Try the kitchen."
—Henny Youngman

When my husband comes home, if the kids are still alive, I figure I've done my job. —Roseanne Barr

I hate housework. You make the beds, you do the dishes— and six months later you have to start all over again.
—Joan Rivers

Cleaning your house before the kids have stopped growing is like shoveling the walk before it stops snowing.
—Phyllis Diller

My mama was afraid to leave dirty dishes in the sink overnight. If a burglar broke in, she would have been embarrassed. —Sam Levenson

★　★　★　★　★

When my wife came back from vacation, I knew she'd be mad at the mess the house was in, so I had the kids make up a sign that said, "Welcome Home, Mommy." And we hung it where the dining room used to be.

— ★ —

Our house is such a mess, the termites tried to have us exterminated.

My house is such a mess that the neighbors got a petition up against us. Now we all have to wipe our feet before *going out*.

The walls in our house are half-clean. Our neighbor takes care of the side that faces her.

I won't say my house is a mess, but have you ever seen a fly land in a cloud of dust?

My kids always leave the bathroom a mess. When they take a bath, they leave a ring around the room.

A lot of people think our bathroom has green carpeting in it. That's moss.

My son has a toy boat that he takes in the bathtub with him. It has done more harm than the real Battleship Missouri. That's because I have never accidentally sat down on the real Battleship Missouri.

I always make my children clean their own room. It's good discipline for them, and besides, I'm two years behind in cleaning the rest of the house.

Last week I went into my son's room and found a big, hairy clump of dirt. It was a friend helping him with his homework.

My son collects all kinds of junk—and fast. The first time I cleaned his room, I found the previous owners trying to find their way out.

— ★ —

My daughter's room is crammed full of stuffed animals. If you accidentally fall down in there, you could be cushioned to death.

— ★ —

MAN AROUND THE HOUSE

My husband is so useless, it's hard for me to be romantic with him. I get down on the floor next to him and say, "If you love me, blink your eyes." —Phyllis Diller

I'm an ordinary sort of fellow—42 around the chest, 42 around the waist, 96 around the golf course, and a nuisance around the house. —Groucho Marx

★ ★ ★ ★ ★

People say it's nice to have a man around the house. Not my husband—he's just something else that has to be dusted.

— ★ —

My husband does absolutely nothing around the house. I get the feeling I married a knickknack.

— ★ —

Asking my husband to do something is like talking to the walls, except the walls are standing up.

My husband hasn't mowed the front lawn in so long that the only way the mailman can get to the front door is to swing on a vine.

My husband does absolutely nothing around the house. It's like being married to a giant Tinkertoy.

My husband is the world's greatest procrastinator. At our wedding, the minister said, "You may now kiss the bride." My husband said, "Tomorrow."

My husband does absolutely nothing around the house. I searched all over him for a cord. I figured maybe you have to plug him in.

My husband is embarrassing. All he ever does is sleep. Sometimes I smear him with grease and slide him under the car just to fool the neighbors.

My husband watches so much football on the weekends, his skin is starting to break out in Astroturf.

My husband spends a lot of time sleeping on the floor. We thought he was missing once, then we discovered we had just carpeted over him.

NEAT NEIGHBORS

Have I got a neat neighbor. She's so neat she puts paper under the cuckoo clock.   —Henny Youngman

My next-door neighbor is so neat, when her husband gets up at three in the morning to go to the bathroom, he returns and finds that the bed has been made.
                              —Milton Berle

★ ★ ★ ★ ★

I live next door to the neatest housekeeper in the world. If she knew then that man came from dirt, she would have refused to be born.

This lady is so neat, when you ring her doorbell it sprays you with DDT.

— ★ —

This lady is a cleanliness fanatic. Her welcome mat is filled with Lysol.

— ★ —

This lady keeps her house so clean that dust has to request permission to land.

COOKING

★

Me a cook? I always threatened my children with, "If you don't shape up, you go to bed with dinner."
—Erma Bombeck

I miss my wife's cooking—as often as I can.
—Henny Youngman

I know I'm a lousy cook, but I never realized how bad until the other night when I caught the dog calling Chicken Delight.
—Joan Rivers

I'll give you an idea how bad my cooking is—last Christmas the family chipped in together and bought me an oven that flushes.
—Phyllis Diller

My wife's cooking is so bad, I went in the kitchen once and saw a cockroach eating a Tums.
—Slappy White

★ ★ ★ ★ ★

Her favorite dessert recipe begins: "Take the juice from one bottle of Pepto Bismol. . . ."

— ★ —

His specialty is dumplings with the accent on the "dump."

— ★ —

Her cooking keeps flies away better than a Shell No-Pest strip.

— ★ —

If you ever want to get revenge on the ants, bring some of his cooking on your next picnic.

Her cooking melts in your mouth. Oh, it may take two or three days, but it melts in your mouth.

His cooking is so bad, his garbage disposal has an ulcer.

Her cooking is so bad that the silverware in her house is imprinted with the Surgeon General's warning.

She's not a real good cook. She can take even the most inexpensive piece of meat and turn it into a lethal weapon.

He asked the family to buy him a chef's hat. They got him a black hood.

I'm a pretty bad cook. If I had cooked the first Thanksgiving meal for the Indians, General Custer might be alive today.

I'll never forget my first meal as a young bride. My husband won't either. He's still being treated for it.

The family knows how dangerous my cooking is. Why else would Grace last 45 minutes?

I don't mind my wife serving leftovers once in a while, but from World War II?

My wife is such a bad cook, we have cold cereal for breakfast every morning. She prepares it the night before.

My wife's cooking is so bad, we have holes in our screen door where the flies go out.

One time I saw her give the leftovers to the dog. And the dog gave them to the cat.

Nobody wants to eat her food. In her kitchen, the flies swat themselves.

When she serves the family fried chicken, the chicken is the only lucky one at the table.

There is such a buildup of crud in my oven, there is only room to bake a single cupcake. —Phyllis Diller

Sure my mother had an automatic garbage disposal. She would detect unerringly when you plan to go out and put the garbage bag in your hand to take out with you.
—Sam Levenson

Our toaster works on either AC or DC, but not on bread. It has two settings—too soon or too late.

—Sam Levenson

Our kitchen had an electric dishwasher, an electric can opener, an electric garbage disposal. My wife said, "There's so many appliances in here I don't have room to sit down." I bought her an electric chair.

—Henny Youngman

We have a toaster at home that we got from a bank. Every day at three o'clock it stops working.

We have a toaster that we got from a bank. It toasts the bread all right, but you have to fill out a withdrawal slip to get it to pop up.

We have a new juicer and my wife likes to try it out on everything. This morning for breakfast I had bread juice.

I'm not real good in the kitchen. I had to shop all over town for a Cuisinart with training wheels.

We have so many appliances in our kitchen, when we have breakfast all the traffic lights in our town stop working.

My wife has a super new high-powered hair dryer. Yesterday she dried her hair in ten seconds, but now her eyebrows are missing.

We have a new Cuisinart that does everything in the kitchen. It even cries over spilt milk.

My Dad makes his morning coffee in the microwave. Instant coffee is not fast enough for him.

Microwave ovens are so great. Thanks to them, we can now have heartburn without having to wait for it.

You can tell when a husband isn't handy when he asks the man next door how to get blood off a saw. —Milton Berle

★   ★   ★   ★   ★

You put a hammer in my husband's hand, and you've put together two things with roughly the same intelligence.

My husband has a can of nails in the garage with a little note on the top that reads: Pointy side towards wall.

The only time my husband has ever joined two pieces of wood together was when he accidentally hit himself in the head with a 2 × 4.

My husband is no handyman. I asked him to hang a picture for me. He tied a piece of rope around it and kicked a chair from under it.

My husband is not good with tools unless they happen to be a beer can opener.

My husband is dangerous on handyman projects. He has a tool box that's filled to the top—with a screwdriver, a hammer, and Band-Aids.

My husband is such a dangerous handyman, his tool box has a siren on it.

I just had my kitchen redone. It started out when I asked my husband to hang the curtains.

My husband tried to fix our plumbing himself. Now we get our water by mail.

My husband somehow got our plumbing mixed up with the electricity. Now every time I take a shower, all our lights go out.

. . . what's worse than that, our television set leaks.

— ★ —

KING OF THE ROAD

ACT
9

*"I'm having awful car troubles.
The car won't start and
the payments won't stop."*
—Milton Berle

AUTOMOBILES

★

Boy, our new car was a real lemon. The windshield wipers were on the inside—the only time they do any good is when you're backing through a snowstorm with the rear window open.　　　　　**—Phyllis Diller**

When I'm on the highway in my car, just once I'd like to see someone pass me without pointing to my tires.
　　　　　—Rodney Dangerfield

I drove my car up to a toll bridge. The man said, "Fifty cents." I said, "Sold."　　　　　**—Slappy White**

★　　★　　★　　★　　★

They have cars now that talk to you. I don't want a car that talks. When I get stopped by a highway patrolman, I don't want a car that could squeal on me.

Today's cars are aerodynamically designed. Yessir, they're built to sit in traffic jams at high speed.

I must admit I'm very dumb about buying used cars. I kick the doors and slam the tires.

— ★ —

I had a car once that was a real lemon. On this car even the ashtrays didn't work.

Talk about lemons. Most cars have a spare tire in the trunk; this car had a tow truck.

I bought one car that was a real mistake. The first time I parked it on the street, a cop gave me a ticket for littering.

I had a car once that was such a lemon, when I'd pull into a service station, I'd get a tank of gas and a six-pack of motor oil.

I had one automobile that was built so badly, it didn't come with a warranty—it came with an apology.

Our new car was such a lemon, the only thing we got with it that still works is the coupon book.

I bought one used car that was such a lemon, when I drove it home, the car got home a half hour before the motor did.

I bought a car once that I knew was going to be a lot of trouble because it was delivered by Parcel Post.

. . . it took me three days to get the stamps off the windshield.

. . . and the spare tire came with nine cents postage due.

DRIVING

To my wife, double parking means on top of another car.
—Dave Barry

My wife doesn't stop for red lights anymore. She says, "If you've seen one or two, you've seen 'em all."
—Dave Barry

Never lend your car to anyone to whom you have given birth.   —Erma Bombeck

My wife called me. She said, "There's water in the carburetor." I said, "Where's the car?" She said, "In the lake."
—Henny Youngman

The best way to stop the noise in the car is to let her drive.   —Milton Berle

Fang is a typical husband. When I drive he complains about every telephone pole I hit. But, does he ever compliment me on the ones I miss?   —Phyllis Diller

★　★　★　★　★

This guy drove so fast his driver's license was issued by the FAA.

. . . He graduated from the Evel Knievel School of Driving.

I'll never forget the first ticket I ever got—$30 for passing on the wrong side of a subway train.

I got my driver's license by default. They never found the officer who gave me my test.

I'm such a bad driver, I had three accidents just taking the written driver's test.

I refused to take the eye exam at my driver's test. I figured: why should I? I never look where I'm going anyway.

My wife is such a bad driver, when she goes into the garage, the car puts its tail pipe between its legs.

When my wife drives, the little statue climbs off the dashboard and crawls into the glove compartment.

One day I came home complaining about the car. I said, "Do you know that's the third clutch I've had to replace." My wife said, "Don't blame me. I never use it."

My uncle is a maniac on the freeways. He only gets about six miles to the cuss word.

— ★ —

The other day my uncle honked at twelve cars, shook his fist at seven, made obscene gestures at four, and cursed three— and he hadn't pulled out of the driveway yet.

— ★ —

The way people drive today, half of them should be pulled over by police, and the other half should be pulled over by their psychiatrists.

Driving changes people. Everybody on the road today is a regular "Dr. Jekyll and Mr. Goodwrench."

I've actually seen drivers roll down their windows and curse passing motorists—from cars that were being towed.

Years ago you had to roll down your window to curse a passing motorist; nowadays you can call him on your car phone.

— ★ —

I saw a guy drive right through a red light the other day, and the guy behind him got angry because he didn't drive through it fast enough.

— ★ —

TRAFFIC

★

Traffic was so heavy it was bumper to bumper. A man pushed a cigarette lighter in, and the woman in the car in front said, "Ouch!" —Henny Youngman

The only way to solve the traffic problem is to pass a law that only paid-for cars are allowed to use the highways. —Will Rogers

The traffic is so heavy in New York's midtown that one day I saw three cars chasing the same pedestrian.

—Jan Murray

Traffic was so bad on the freeway the other day—on the way home I had to stop three times to make car payments.

The roads are getting packed nowadays. The only way you can change lanes now is to buy the car next to you.

Traffic used to be bumper to bumper; now it's worse. It's windshield to windshield.

It used to take three hours by horse-drawn buggy to go from one end of the city to the other. Today it takes you that long just to get on the freeway.

People don't want to be in traffic that much—it's just that there's no place else to go when you can't find a parking place.

The law says there should be five car lengths between you and the car in front of you. In order to get that, you have to talk at least four people into staying home.

Traffic is getting so bad nowadays that you can now change a flat without losing your place in line.

I remember how embarrassed people used to get when their car stalled on the highway. Nowadays, it's no problem; you just blend in with the normal traffic flow.

The only way to get home on time in today's traffic is to take the day off.

Traffic is so congested, a pedestrian nowadays is someone in a hurry.

Cars are jammed so close together, they may soon sell gas with deodorant in it.

I watched the young couple in front of me necking all the way home on the freeway. They were in separate cars.

Traffic is so bad nowadays that even people who are going to stay home have to leave early.

Traffic is so congested today, if you throw a hubcap during rush hour, it'll probably get to work before you do.

There's no courtesy on the highways today. One man put his arm out the window to signal a lane change and somebody stole his watch.

Traffic is really congested on our highways. One Cadillac pulled over to the side of the road, opened its hood, and two Volkswagens drove out.

I WONDER WHERE MY LUGGAGE WENT

ACT
10

*"If you look like your passport photo,
you're too ill to travel."*
—Will Kommen

TRAVEL

★
....

*Travel is very educational. I can now say "Kaopectate" in
seven different languages.* —Bob Hope

*Actually, I'm an advocate of separate vacations—the
children's and ours.* —Erma Bombeck

*They spell it "Vinci" and pronounce it "Vinchy"; for-
eigners always spell better than they pronounce.*
—Mark Twain

*I travelled to China. Boy, there ought to be a law against
making an ocean that wide.* —Will Rogers

*She was so ugly customs wouldn't let her enter the coun-
try without a crate.* —Milton Berle

★ ★ ★ ★ ★

He used to do so much travelling he never needed a plane. He
had a business suit made with a fuel tank added.

— ★ —

He flies around the world so much, at his last physical they
found traces of feathers.

— ★ —

He travels so much that he has to wait till the morning paper
comes to find out what city he's in.

— ★ —

He's done so much travelling that every time he sits down he puts his seat back and tray table to its upright and locked position.

— ★ —

I have jet lag. That's when you arrive and your luggage is in better shape than you are.

— ★ —

Jet lag is nature's way of making you look like your passport photo.

— ★ —

I travel a lot. I go to about half as many places as my luggage does.

— ★ —

I checked my luggage last week. The guy tore off the stubs and said, "Here are your lottery tickets."

— ★ —

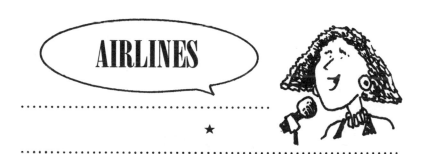

....

★

....

I flew over here on the Concorde. That plane is so fast it gives you an extra couple of hours to look for your luggage. —Bob Hope

If the Lord had wanted people to fly, He would have made it simpler for people to get to the airport. —Milton Berle

I don't fly on account of my religion—I'm a devout coward. —Henny Youngman

I was on an airplane. The pilot came running down the aisle with a parachute strapped to his back. He said, "Don't be alarmed, but we're having a little trouble with the landing gear. I'm gonna run on ahead and warn them at the airport." —Slappy White

People are afraid of airplanes. I got in the ticket line behind an honest man once. He said to the clerk, "Give me two chances to Pittsburgh."

I don't worry about flying. I figure there can't be anything on the plane more dangerous than the airline food.

If it weren't for airlines, we'd be up to our necks in honey-roasted peanuts.

Flying is getting very expensive nowadays. The other day I saw a bird riding a bicycle.

— ★ —

What a hotel: The towels were so big and fluffy, you could hardly close your suitcase. —Henny Youngman

There was only one hotel in my hometown. It wasn't much, but at least it had a bridal suite. It was the room with the lock on the door. —Herb Shriner

My hotel room was so small, every time I put the key in the lock, I broke the window. —Milton Berle

My hotel room was so small, I couldn't brush my teeth sideways. —Milton Berle

I once had a hotel room that was so small it had removable doorknobs—just in case you wanted to bend over. —Fred Allen

Hotels are getting bigger and bigger. I called for room service at one of them and my meal arrived by UPS.

Some of the hotels are too big. It's annoying to have to carry your passport every time you want to go down to the lobby.

I went to one hotel and just wanted to stay overnight. They wouldn't let me. They said that wouldn't give me enough time to get to my room.

This is a very big hotel. They give two weather reports here—one for inside the hotel and one for outside.

This is really an immense building. I don't know whether this hotel has a manager or a governor.

This hotel is so big, I went up to the desk and said, "Do I ask for a reservation or apply for citizenship?"

This is a giant hotel. Room service is a long-distance call.

This hotel is really immense. It's the only one I've ever seen where the bellhops are on horseback.

This hotel is so large, before they carry your luggage to your room, they ask if there are any perishables in them.

I stayed in one hotel that was so chintzy, I had to carry my own bags up to my room. I wouldn't have minded if I was a bigger tipper.

This hotel was very cheap, but they still have a change of linen every day. Room 301 changes with room 303, room 302 changes with room 304. . . .

Nobody at this hotel had any self-confidence. The guy who operated the elevator had to stop three times to ask directions.

— ★ —

"Quit worrying about your health.
It'll go away."
—Robert Orben

HEALTH

★

It's no longer a question of staying healthy. It's a question of finding a sickness that you like. —Jackie Mason

Health nuts are going to feel stupid someday, lying in hospitals dying of nothing. —Redd Fox

I personally stay away from health foods. At my age, I need all the preservatives I can get. —George Burns

The only way to keep your health is to eat what you don't want, drink what you don't like, and do what you'd rather not. —Mark Twain

There's a lot of people in this world who spend so much time watching their health that they haven't the time to enjoy it. —Josh Billings

★   ★   ★   ★   ★

I've never been sick a day in my life. Nights I get a little nauseous, but days never.

— ★ —

An apple a day keeps the doctor away; an onion a day keeps everyone away.

— ★ —

It's better to be healthy than wise. If you're sick, it costs you money; but you can be stupid for free.

— ★ —

If you've got your health, you've got everything. And if you don't have your health, sooner or later your doctor has everything.

— ★ —

We are so health conscious today. But what good is health? It can't buy money.

— ★ —

A friend of mine went to a new health club and lost four pounds immediately. And that was only his first payment.

— ★ —

My uncle ate nothing but oat bran every day of his life, and he lived a healthy, happy life up until the day he fell in love and tried to marry the horse who won the Kentucky Derby.

— ★ —

My grandfather always used to ask me, "What's more important, your money or your health?" I'd say, "My health." He'd say, "Great, can you lend me 20 bucks?"

— ★ —

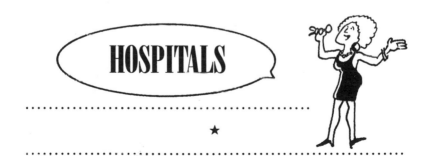

HOSPITALS

★

GEORGE: *Gracie, did the nurse ever happen to drop you on your head when you were a baby?*
GRACIE: *Oh, no, we couldn't afford a nurse, my mother had to do it.*   —Burns and Allen

When you get your hospital bill, you understand why surgeons wear masks in the operating room.

—Sam Levenson

Hospitals are weird. They put you in a private room and then give you a public gown. —Milton Berle

After two days in the hospital, I took a turn for the nurse.

—W. C. Fields

I had a very tough nurse in the hospital. She had a black belt in nursing.

A hospital is an institution that is dedicated to the cure of disease—and modesty.

I can't figure out which covers less—the hospital gown or my insurance company.

Most hospitals have two accident wards. One of them is the kitchen.

But look on the bright side. The food they serve makes the medicine taste good.

Hospitals now even have "outpatient surgery." You come in and have your surgery and go home the same day. They're finding out you get cured faster when you don't have to eat hospital food.

DOCTORS, DENTISTS & SHRINKS

Never go to a doctor whose office plants have died.
—Erma Bombeck

I'm getting fed up with my doctor. He told me I should keep smoking if I wanted to stop chewing gum.
—Rodney Dangerfield

My wife wanted a face lift. The doctors couldn't do that, but for $80 they lowered her body. —Henny Youngman

One time I went to the doctor and told him I had a ringing in my ear. He said, "Don't answer it."
—Rodney Dangerfield

My doctor is wonderful. Once, in 1955, when I couldn't afford an operation, he touched up the X-rays.
—Joey Bishop

I went to a psychoanalyst for years—and it helped—now I get rejected from a much better class of girls.
—Woody Allen

My dentist just put in a tooth to match my other teeth. It has three cavities. —Milton Berle

I'm in Pretty Good Shape for the Shape I'm In   103

The doctor who performed my surgery is at this banquet tonight. I happened to glance over at him during the meal and his wife was cutting his meat for him.

The doctor told me my operation was fairly routine and not at all complicated. I told him to remember that when he makes out the bill.

My doctor is very conservative. If he doesn't need the money, he doesn't operate.

My doctor told me this operation was absolutely necessary. I said, "For what?" He said, "To send my kids through college."

My doctor gave me a needle that was the biggest thing I ever saw in my life. Well, it was the biggest thing I ever saw until I got his bill for it.

My family doctor is just like my family dog. Neither one of them will come when you call.

My doctor's very good. He guarantees you'll live to be as old as some of the magazines in his waiting room.

I could never figure out why my dentist had travel magazines in his waiting room. Then one day he hit a nerve and I jumped all the way to Cleveland.

My dentist went to dental school in Texas. He keeps drilling until he strikes oil.

— ★ —

Dentists are different from anybody else. For one thing, they're the only people who will invite you to spit in their sink.

My psychiatrist, he found out I have two personalities—so he charged me twice as much.

. . . I paid him half and said, "Get the rest from the other guy."

I told the psychiatrist I thought everybody hated me because I was so good-looking. He said, "You don't need a psychiatrist; you need a mirror."

I told the psychiatrist I keep hearing strange voices in my ear. He said, "Where do you want to hear them?"

I went to a psychiatrist for years to get my head on straight. After all that time and money, I found out it was only my tie that was on crooked.

— ★ —

I've been on a constant diet for the last two decades. I've lost a total of 789 pounds. By all accounts, I should be hanging from a charm bracelet.   —Erma Bombeck

My wife is a light eater. As soon as it's light, she starts eating.
                                                    —Henny Youngman

I once went on a three-week diet and lost twenty-one days.
                                                    —Jack E. Leonard

I found there was only one way to look thin—hang out with fat people.
                                                    —Rodney Dangerfield

My wife came home one day and said, "Look, honey, I lost 15 pounds." I said, "If you look behind you, you'll find them."
                                                    —Slappy White

They have a new diet now where you eat nothing but garlic and onions. Everybody stays so far away from you that from a distance you look thinner.

I'm on a diet now that guarantees I'll lose a pound a day. I'll say good-bye now because by Christmas I'll be gone completely.

. . . If you stay on this diet long enough, you need staples to hold your socks up.

My uncle once went on a total seafood diet. He was doing pretty good, too, until he drowned one day trying to get lunch.

You know you should go on a diet when you buy something marked "one size fits all" and your name is printed on the label as one of the exceptions.

Some of those snack foods have so many chemicals in them you can't even buy them without a prescription.

. . . I compromise. I buy them, but I keep them in my medicine cabinet.

— ★ —

Some of the hamburgers they serve in fast food restaurants are very thin. If you hold them up to the light, you can read the menu through them.

— ★ —

Our lemonade today is made up of nothing but chemicals. The only place you can get real lemonade is in furniture polish.

. . . our dining-room table eats better than we do.

— ★ —

They se ve food full of chemicals. I looked at the trash cans behind a fast food restaurant. Fake flies were buzzing around them.

— ★ —

EXERCISE

★

I take my exercise acting as pallbearer at the funerals of those who exercised regularly. —Mark Twain

I am pushing 60—that's enough exercise for me.
—Mark Twain

My wife went to one of those gymnasiums and lost 37 pounds. One of those machines tore her leg off.

—Slappy White

I exercise daily to keep my figure. I keep patting my hand against the bottom of my chin. It works, too—I have the thinnest fingers in town.   —Totie Fields

I don't exercise at all. I figure if God meant for us to touch our toes, He would have put them farther up our body.

I don't want a perfect body. I've had this one for so long, I've grown attached to it.

Some runners in our neighborhood get up and go out jogging at 4:30 in the morning. If I'm ever up at that time of day, I want to be coming home.

There are so many joggers out on the streets in the mornings that cars have to use the sidewalks.

If God wanted us to run down the street, He would have made us with turn signals.

You have to be careful about jogging. The doctor told a neighbor of mine that he should jog three miles every morning. Last we heard from him, he was in Pittsburgh.

OUR WORLD & WELCOME TO IT

ACT 12

*"Let's face it, our world
is the best place to live on earth."*
—Gene Perret

WEATHER

★

It's been so cold this winter, the Golden Girls had to be jump-started. —Bob Hope

It was so cold I saw a politician with his hands in his own pockets. —Henny Youngman

Freezing people for the future isn't a new idea. Landlords discovered it years ago. —Pat Cooper

It was so cold I saw a polar bear wearing a grizzly. —Milton Berle

The coldest winter I ever spent was a summer in San Francisco. —Mark Twain

It was so hot out today, I saw a Dalmatian with his spots on the ground. —Pat McCormick

★　★　★　★　★

If you want to get an idea of how hot it is, try cleaning your oven the next time from the inside.

. . . while you're roasting a turkey.

— ★ —

It's so hot the grapes in the Fruit-of-the-Loom label turned to raisins.

— ★ —

It's really been hot. I saw a dog chasing a cat in Beverly Hills the other day and it was so hot, both of their chauffeurs passed out.

This heat is tough on everybody. I saw a flock of birds heading north today and they were hitchhiking.

. . . and they would only accept rides in air-conditioned cars.

Soon we're going to have four seasons—summer, simmer, broil, and bake.

It was really hot today. At the Hollywood Wax Museum, John Wayne melted down to the size of Mickey Rooney.

It was really hot today. In fact, one poor dog had his tongue out so far his tail disappeared.

It's been pretty cold lately. The other day I saw a dog chasing a cat and they were both ice skating.

It was so cold, everything was freezing. Cows were giving cream by the scoop.

It was so cold in New York, the Statue of Liberty was holding the torch *under* her dress.

Last night, it was so cold I fell out of bed and cracked my pajamas.

In cold weather like this, you're constantly numb. If you sat on a tack, you wouldn't notice it until the spring thaw.

— ★ —

It's so cold around here that everything is frozen. I had to wear a bullet-proof vest to take a shower.

— ★ —

It was so cold last week, my grandpa's teeth were chattering—and they were home on the dresser.

— ★ —

I have a real good blanket that's especially made for this cold weather. It has three settings: warm, warmer, and the life you save may be your own.

. . . It has a fourth setting, too, but if you put it on that, you need a pardon from the Governor to turn it off.

— ★ —

It was so cold we circled the airport six times. It took that long for the plane to get the courage to set its tail down on the frozen runway.

— ★ —

Everything in the country was covered with snow. I was sure glad when our plane rolled to a stop in New York—especially since we had landed in Chicago.

— ★ —

It's been so cold lately people have to use an ice pick to get comfortable on their water beds.

— ★ —

It's been so cold lately the Abominable Snowman moved to Palm Springs.

— ★ —

People are trying everything to keep warm. General Electric has even come out with a new crock pot that sleeps two.

This cold weather is really something. The bathroom in my hotel room was equipped with hot and cold running ice cubes.

On Groundhog's Day, if the groundhog comes out of his hole and sees his shadow, it means six more weeks of winter. It's been so cold this year, he came out of his hole and bought a condominium in Florida.

It's been so cold lately that it's costing doctors a lot of money. They have to hire four assistants to get people to strip to the waist.

This is the worst drought in history. I saw a woman in the supermarket yesterday buying bottled dust.

This drought is so bad that at most of the prisons, they're serving the prisoners bread and bread.

There's such a drought that some restaurants are charging for water. There was a big argument in Beverly Hills the other day. One customer was angry because they brought him the wrong year.

— ★ —

Water is so scarce right now I read where two fish just bought themselves a mobile home.

— ★ —

The scarcity of water is causing real problems. Last week our porch caught fire and the firemen had to blow it out.

— ★ —

The government says we're not allowed to water our lawns. Yesterday four earthworms came to my door and asked to borrow a cup of water.

— ★ —

The drought is real bad. I turned on my faucet the other day and an I.O.U. came out.

— ★ —

★

Those earthquakes in California are something. It's frightening when your bedroom gets up and goes down to breakfast before you do.

—Bob Hope

After the earthquake, my house is still up on the hill, but my view just got lowered. —Bob Hope

My family and I have come up with a course of action for an earthquake. At the first tremor, we get out of bed calmly, stand in a doorway, and start screaming. Maybe you know our system under another name—panic.
—Milton Berle

I don't know if that was a strong quake, but my zip code changed three times. —Milton Berle

We have a lot of quakes in California. Half the time you don't even have to stir your own coffee in the morning. Mother Nature does it for you.

One Los Angeles television station offered an "Earthquake Survival Guide." I sent in a self-addressed stamped envelope, and they sent me a map to Kansas.

One guy was getting a tattoo when an earthquake hit. He now has his girlfriend's name written across his chest . . . around his back, and down his left leg.

There are a lot of earthquakes in southern California. You know those addresses they paint on the curb in front of your house? In southern California, they do them in pencil.

Experts say the way your animal behaves can sometimes help predict an earthquake. The night before the last earthquake hit, my poodle packed a suitcase and headed back to France.

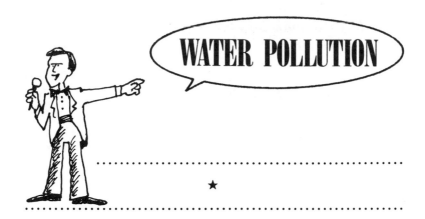

WATER POLLUTION

All the drinks in Hawaii have something floating in them. It's kind of like our water back in Los Angeles.

—Bob Hope

★ ★ ★ ★ ★

Our waters are polluted. Last week a half dozen saltwater fish came to my house and asked to use the pool.

Our fish are so filled with mercury they can take their own temperature.

The water is so polluted not too many people fish anymore. One guy did. He caught a sea bass wearing a gas mask.

There's so much oil in our waters nowadays, you can catch two kinds of tuna—regular or unleaded.

In California they have no-smoking signs on the beach. There's so much oil in the water that the ocean could catch fire.

Last week a whale washed up on the beach. He claimed he slipped out of the water.

— ★ —

In California, people wipe their feet when they come *out* of the ocean.

— ★ —

All of our waters are filthy. Recently someone reported that they discovered water under Lake Erie.

— ★ —

AIR POLLUTION

....
★
....

There's so much pollution in the air now that if it weren't for our lungs, there'd be no place to put it all.

—Robert Orben

Fight air pollution—inhale. —Red Buttons

I don't like all this fresh air. I'm from Los Angeles. I don't trust any air I can't see. —Bob Hope

The smog was so bad, I opened my mouth to yawn and chipped a tooth! —Bob Hope

★ ★ ★ ★ ★

Nowadays, you get up in the morning, open the window, take a deep breath, and you're in no condition to do your exercises.

People nowadays wake up and go outside to have a *bite* of fresh air.

But it's still a thrill to spot the first robin of spring—having a coughing fit on your lawn.

People on this earth say God is dead. I don't think so. I think He's just staying in Heaven for reasons of His health.

I had a friend who went to the doctor to have his heart checked. The doctor put the stethoscope on his chest and said, "Take a deep breath." His heart was fine; the deep breath killed him.

New York is working very hard to clear up their air pollution. They want to have nothing but healthy people being mugged in Central Park.

The politicians are getting active in environmental safety. They want to remove from our air, smog, auto emissions, toxic chemicals, and acid rain. If they take all that out of the air, what's going to hold the birds up?

I do wish they would eliminate acid rain. I'm getting tired of lugging around that lead umbrella.

Air pollution is commonplace nowadays. Everyone's eyes water so much, they're selling contact lenses that come with windshield wipers.

LIFE & ITS AFTER-EFFECTS

ACT 13

"Life is what happens to you while you're busy making other plans."
—John Lennon

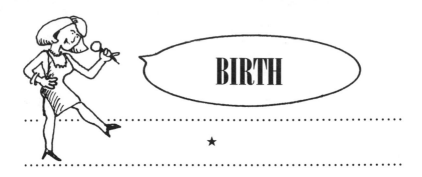

BIRTH

★

I was so ugly when I was born the doctor slapped my mother. —Henny Youngman

Red Skelton ran into an old friend from the town where he was born. "Red," he exclaimed, "you sure have put on a lot of weight." Red replied, "Yeah, I only weighed seven pounds when I was born." —Red Skelton

Once my husband said to me, "I'm going to have some coffee. Do you want me to put some hot water on for you?" I thought that was the least he could do considering I was giving birth. —Phyllis Diller

When I was born, I was so surprised I couldn't talk for a year and a half. —Gracie Allen

I was born modest; not all over, but in spots. —Mark Twain

★ ★ ★ ★ ★

I was born in Philadelphia. I wanted to be near my mother.

My birth must have come as quite a surprise. I didn't even have a chance to dress for it.

I don't know why I was born in a hospital. Up until then I was never sick a day in my life.

— ★ —

I don't remember much about my birth. I was only a child at the time.

I weighed six pounds, eight ounces when I was born. I eat more than that now for lunch.

After I was born, the doctor sent my father a bill for $500. I don't know why—Mom and I did all the work.

My father was so happy when I was born he rushed out to tell all his friends. We expect him back any day now.

— ★ —

My Dad said I was the cutest baby he'd ever seen except that I had no nose. Then he discovered he was holding me upside down and backwards.

— ★ —

OLD AGE

★

I've been around for awhile. When I was a boy, the Dead Sea was only sick. —George Burns

You know you're old when everything hurts, and what doesn't hurt, doesn't work. —George Burns

The secret of staying young is to live honestly, eat slowly and lie about your age.　　　　　　　　—Lucille Ball

I have everything now I had 20 years ago—except now it's all lower.　　　　　　　　—Gypsy Rose Lee

One nice thing about old age—you can whistle while you brush your teeth.　　　　　　　　—Jack Carter

Life begins at forty, but so does arthritis and the habit of telling the same story three times to the same person.
　　　　　　　　—Sam Levenson

I have "Old-Timers Disease." I don't forget things; I lose interest in them.

I think people should enjoy old age. It's the one thing they can do better than the youngsters.

I'm going through my second childhood right now. It's my fourth trip through.

Age is only a state of mind—that is, provided you have one left.

After a certain age, the only things you're allowed to do are things you either don't want to do or have already forgotten how to do.

I'm not ashamed of growing older. I always tell people my correct age on my birthday—when it rolls around every three or four years.

I know a fellow who is so old that he has one of the few Social Security cards left with the number written in Roman numerals.

He's so old that when he plays golf, he doesn't have to yell "Fore." His bones creaking warns the foursome ahead of him.

He's hit that time of life when if you blow out all the candles on your cake, you not only get your wish, but you also get a hernia.

I was always taught to respect my elders. But it's getting harder and harder—to find one.

You know you're getting on in years when your life flashes before your eyes and you fall asleep during it.

Older Americans are really in good shape. We used to offer our seats to old ladies on a bus. Now they're in good enough shape to *take* them.

They are really keeping young. Yesterday I saw four old ladies helping a Boy Scout across the street.

. . . it took four of them because he didn't want to go.

It's nice that we got our older citizens out of rocking chairs and wheelchairs. Now they're starting to hang out in groups on street corners.

— ★ —

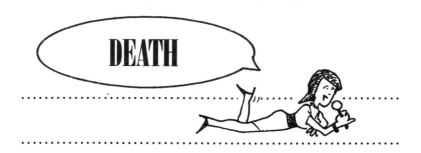

DEATH

MAN: *Do you realise that every time I draw a mortal breath an immortal soul passes on into eternity?*

MARK TWAIN: *Ever try cloves?* —Mark Twain

Dying is not popular; it's never caught on. That's understandable; it's bad for the complexion.

—George Burns

This guy dies and leaves the shortest will. It said, "Being in my sound mind, I spent my money."

—Henny Youngman

We usually meet all our relatives only at funerals where someone always observes, "Too bad we can't get together more often." —Sam Levenson

I'm not afraid to die, I just don't want to be there when it happens. —Woody Allen

★　★　★　★　★

Death is one way of putting an end to all that junk mail.

Death is a way of saying: Yesterday was the last day of the rest of your life.

Death is nature's way of saying, "Hold all my calls."

Death is the last thing everybody does, and it's the first thing a lot of them do correctly.

— ★ —

Death is the ultimate in packing light for a trip.

— ★ —

Death is nature's way of missing the last exit before the toll booth.

— ★ —

SPIRITUAL MATTERS

★

God sneezed. What could I say to Him?
—Henny Youngman

I believe our Heavenly Father invented man because He was disappointed in the monkey. —Mark Twain

If only God would give me a clear sign! Like making a large deposit in my name at a Swiss bank.
—Woody Allen

Definition of a dead atheist: All dressed up and nowhere to go. —Woody Woodbury

The reason God made man before woman was because He didn't want any suggestions. —Sam Levenson

God knows all things. He'd be a great person to have help you with your homework, wouldn't He?

I know God is up there even though I can't see Him. In Los Angeles, I know the sky is up there even though I can't see that either.

How can some people say God is dead? We're not even sure about Elvis.

I once prayed in a hotel and they charged me a 75-cent long-distance service charge.

Sometimes technology can be a detriment. I tried to pray the other day and got God's answering machine.

. . . My preacher told me not to worry about it. If my prayer had been really important, they would have beeped Him.

INDEX

Age, 122, 123
Airlines, 47, 95–96
Air pollution, 117–118
Allen, Fred, 11, 16, 24, 38, 39, 58
Allen, Gracie, 17, 26; see also Burns & Allen
Allen, Woody, 10, 22, 52, 54, 69, 103, 124, 125
Amsterdam, Morey, 26, 39
Appearance, 53–55
Appliances, electrical, 82
Atheist, 125
Automobiles, see Cars

Babies, 101, 120, 121
Baby-sitter, 16
Bachelors, 66–67
Baldness, 60–62
Ball, Lucille, 122
Barbers, 62–63
Barr, Roseanne, 74
Barry, Dave, 59, 88
Baseball, 30–32
Bathroom, 72, 75
Beauty, 55–56
Benchley, Robert, 20
Benny, Jack, 45, 46
Bergen, Edgar, 22
Berle, Milton, 17, 24, 30, 32, 38, 41, 44, 60, 61, 66, 71, 78, 83, 85, 88, 94, 95, 97, 102, 103, 110, 115
Beverly Hills, 73, 114
Billings, Josh, 12, 43, 100
Birth, 120–121
Bishop, Joey, 72, 103
Bodybuilders, 59–60
Bombeck, Erma, 9, 16, 28, 33, 50, 55, 58, 64, 79, 88, 94, 103, 105
Bores, 39–40
Birds, 118

Boxing, 35–36
Brains, 26
Breath, bad, 124
Brenner, David, 53
Burns & Allen, 18, 72, 101; see also Allen, Gracie, and Burns, George
Burns, George, 11, 34, 67, 100, 121, 124
Buttons, Red, 117

Caesar, Sid, 61
Cars, 68, 69, 71, 85–92
Carter, Jack, 122
Cheapskates, 45–47
Chemicals, in food, 107
Childcare, 73
Childhood, 14–15
Children, 16, 75
Clothes, 50–52
Cold, 110–113
Comedian, 11, 12
Conceit, 38–39
Cooking, 79–81
Cooper, Pat, 110
Costs, high, 96
Couch potatoes, 42–44
Crazies, 47–48
Cuisinart, 82, 83
Customs, 94

Dangerfield, Rodney, 14, 16, 22, 30, 35, 67, 68, 86, 103, 106
Dating, 67–68
Dentists, 104–105
Diets, 105–107
Diller, Phyllis, 16, 20, 24, 42, 46, 50, 52, 53, 55, 56, 58, 63, 69, 72, 74, 76, 79, 81, 86, 88, 120
Death, 124–125
Doctors, 11, 15, 100–105, 118, 121
Dogs, 19, 20, 24, 44, 61
Dressed, worst, 52–53

Driving, 88–90
Drought, 113–114
Dummies, 24–25
Durante, Jimmy, 53
Earthquakes, 114–115
Eaters, big, 56–57
Education, 22–23
Egomaniacs, 38–39
Exercise, 107–108, 117

Families, 13–20
Fashion, 50–51
Fatness, 54
Fields, Totie, 57, 108
Fields, W. C., 13, 43, 102
Fish, 116
Food, 102, 107
Football, 23, 28–30, 77
Ford, Jerry, 34, 35
Fox, Redd, 100
Funeral, 45, 51, 107, 124

Gabor, Zsa Zsa, 69
Genius, 39, 47
Gleason, Jackie, 58
God, 118, 125, 126
Golden Girls, 110
Golf, 33–34, 123
Grouches, 44–45
Groundhog's Day, 113
Gymnasiums, 108

Hair, 60–64
Handyman, 83–84
Health, 99–101, 118
Heat, 110, 111
Hershfield, Harry, 16
Hockey, 32–33
Home, 71–84
Hope, Bob, 10, 17, 28, 34, 35, 59, 94, 95, 110, 114, 115, 116, 117
Horses, 26
Hospitals, 100–102, 120
Hotels, 96–98, 126
Houses, cost of, 73
Housework, 74–76, 126

Humorist, 11
Husbands, 76–77, 83–84

Insanity, 47–48

Jogging, 108

Kahane, Jackie, 63
Kitchen, 74, 81–83, 102
Kommen, Will, 93

Landlords, 110
Latecomers, 41–42
Laughter, 9, 11–12
Laziness, 42–44
Lee, Gypsy Rose, 122
Lennon, John, 119
Leonard, Jack E., 14, 38, 57, 60, 106
Levenson, Sam, 14, 22, 26, 74, 81, 102, 122, 124, 126
Levant, Oscar, 47
Longworth, Alice Roosevelt, 37
Looks, 49–64
Luck, 10–11
Luggage, 95

Macho, 56
Marriage, 67, 68–70
Martin, Dick, 66
Marx, Groucho, 76
Mason, Jackie, 38, 43, 53, 100
McCormick, Pat, 110
Microwave ovens, 83
Money trouble, 72–73, 101
Murray, Jan, 91
Muscles, 59–60

Neatness, 52, 78

Neighborhoods, 72
Neighbors, 78
Nurse, 101, 102

Old age, 121–123
Operations, 103–104
Orben, Robert, 99, 117
Ovens, 81, 83, 110

Palmer, Arnold, 34
Parents, 14, 15
Parties, 41–42, 45, 51
Perret
  Gene, 109
  Linda, 65
Personality, 39–40
Pets, 19–20
Planes, 47, 94–96; see also Airline
Plumbing, 84
Politicians, 110, 118
Pollution, 116–118
Poverty, 72
Prayer, 126
Presley, Elvis, 126
Prices, 73–74, 96
Procrastination, 77
Psychiatrists, 103, 105

Radner, Gilda, 50
Relatives, 17–19
Rivers, Joan, 23, 57, 74, 79
Rogers, Will, 11, 19, 21, 26, 34, 65, 90, 94
Running, 108

School, 21–26, 42
Shark, 40
Shriner, Herb, 97
Singer, 11
Skelton, Red, 120
Skinnies, 58–59
Smile, 12
Smog, 117

Spiritual matters, 125–126
Sports, 27–36, 73
Stinginess, 45–47
Stock market, 73
Stupidity, 24–25

Termites, 75
Test, driver's, 88–89
Thomas, Danny, 14, 72
Toasters, 82
Traffic jams, 86, 90–92
Travel, 93–98
Twain, Mark, 14, 19, 22, 50, 94, 100, 107, 108, 110, 120, 124, 125

Ugliness, 53

Vacations, 94
Vernon, Jackie, 14
Video games, 17

Water, 114
  pollution, 116–117
Weather, 110–113
Weight, 56–59
White, Slappy, 16, 35, 47, 67, 72, 79, 86, 96, 106, 108
Wilson, Earl, 71
Wolf, 72
Woodbury, Woody, 69, 125

Youngman, Henny, 10, 16, 17, 24, 30, 46, 49, 55, 60, 69, 74, 78, 79, 82, 88, 90, 96, 103, 106, 110, 120, 124, 125
Youth, 122

Zoo, 16